# THOMAS ALLEN

## Strength Training for Teens

*80 Resistance and Isometric Exercises to Improve Strength and Avoid Injury for Sports and Lifelong Fitness*

*Copyright © 2023 by Thomas Allen*

*All rights reserved. No part of this publication may be reproduced, stored, or transmitted in any form or by any means, electronic, mechanical, photocopying, recording, scanning, or otherwise, without written permission from the publisher. It is illegal to copy this book, post it to a website, or distribute it by any other means without permission.*

*Thomas Allen asserts the moral right to be identified as the author of this work.*

*Thomas Allen has no responsibility for the persistence or accuracy of URLs for external or third-party Internet Websites referred to in this publication. He does not guarantee that any content on such Websites is, or will remain, accurate or appropriate.*

*Designations used by companies to distinguish their products are often claimed as trademarks. All brand names and product names used in this book and on its cover are trade names, service marks, trademarks, and registered trademarks of their respective owners. The publishers and the book are not associated with any product or vendor mentioned in this book. None of the companies referenced within the book have endorsed the book.*

*First edition*

# Contents

| | |
|---|---|
| Introduction | 2 |
| Chapter 1: A Foundation of Strength Training | 5 |
| Chapter 2: Safety, Recovery, and Avoiding Injury | 14 |
| Chapter 3: Nutrition for Strength and Growth | 21 |
| Chapter 4: Mental Strength and Well-Being | 28 |
| Chapter 5: Chest Exercises and Techniques | 33 |
| Chapter 6: Arm Exercises and Techniques | 43 |
| Chapter 7: Leg Exercises and Techniques | 53 |
| Chapter 8: Back and Abdominal Exercises and Techniques | 62 |
| Chapter 9: Integrating Strength Training into Sports | 72 |
| Chapter 10: Beyond High School—Lifelong Fitness | 77 |
| Thank you! | 81 |
| References | 82 |

# Introduction

Welcome to the journey of strength—a voyage into the world of teenage fitness that goes beyond the gym, the weights, and the heart of a transformative experience. We're not just talking about lifting weights; we're talking about laying the groundwork for a lifetime of health, vitality, and maybe even a bit of athletic glory.

Together, we will break down the science and secrets of strength training, not as a chore but as a ticket to unlocking your physical and mental potential. So, buckle up because we're about to embark on a mission to understand why strength training is a game-changer for teens. So, what are we covering in this book?

### Importance of Strength Training for Teens

Let's start with an honest talk about why strength training is a secret weapon for teenagers. It's not just about sculpting a physique; it's about building the foundation for a future of resilience and well-being. From bone density to mental fortitude, we're diving into why teens shouldn't just consider strength training; they should embrace it whether they're eyeing the sports field or want to navigate life's challenges with more understanding of how to improve their strength.

### Common Misconceptions and Concerns

But let's clear the air. There are enough myths and half-truths to confuse and mislead even the advanced athlete. We're going to debunk the misconceptions and address the concerns head-on. Are you worried about stunted growth? Concerned about your bikini body turning into the She-Hulk? Relax! We will separate some fact from fiction so that you can approach strength training with confidence, not confusion.

### Proper Technique to Avoid Injury and Choosing Age-Appropriate Routines

Proper technique is not about looking good in the gym but avoiding unnecessary setbacks. We'll break down the moves, focusing on form and function, and highlight the importance of routines tailored for the teenage body. It's not about pushing your limits to impress your friends; it's about pushing the *right way*, ensuring that every press, squat, and curl is a step towards progress, not pain.

### Don't Skip Over the Fundamentals!

One quick note about nutrition, stretching, and technique aren't just buzzwords. They're the heroes of your fitness story. They're the elements that turn a workout into a lifestyle, a routine into a ritual. So, as we examine the world of teen strength training, remember, it's not just about the now; it's about the future you're crafting, one lift at a time.

### Continue the Journey

The final chapter of this book discusses the transition from strength training as a teen to incorporating this into your adult life. After making strength training a reality in your daily life, it is a natural transition with different priorities and goals. I've included a list of references if you want to read more about everything in this book in more detail. So, get ready to lift, learn, and live stronger.

# Chapter 1: A Foundation of Strength Training

You'll face many challenges in life: navigating through a maze of choices, school pressures, and social dynamics that can all be overwhelming. What if I told you that there's a key to unlocking a greater potential? Like leveling up your physical and mental abilities.

Welcome to the world of strength training—a journey into the gym and the core of your physical and mental well-being. So, here's the deal: this book isn't about "shoulds" and "musts"; it's about empowering you with the knowledge to make choices that resonate with your goals.

*Benefits of Strength Training*

Strength training isn't just about pumping iron and flexing muscles; it's about building a robust foundation for the future you. Picture this: enhanced sports performance, a metabolism firing on all cylinders, and a confidence boost that radiates from the inside out. It's not just about looking strong; it's about feeling strong, resilient, and ready to face whatever challenges life throws at you. Imagine every lift, every push, and every pull contributing not just to your physique but to a mental toughness that echoes beyond the gym. It's about more than just the immediate gains; it's about setting the stage for a lifetime of health, vitality, and confidence that extends beyond your High School years.

## Physical Development During Adolescence

But why now? Why is adolescence the golden age for laying this foundation? Let's unpack that. Your body is going through myriad changes—growth spurts, hormones off the chain, and a transformation that's like upgrading to the 2.0 version of yourself. Strength training aligns with this natural rhythm, becoming not just a workout but an integral part of your journey through these years.

As muscles develop, your bones and all other connective tissues strengthen, and your body undergoes a metamorphosis. Strength training becomes the architect, ensuring each movement contributes to the blueprint of physical development. It's not just about getting fit; it's about syncing with the natural progression of your growth, setting the stage for a body that moves with grace, strength, and purpose.

A quick note: I am neither a personal trainer nor a medical doctor. So, this book is intended to be a starting place, refresher, or guide—but should not replace professional medical advice. Ensure you talk to your doctor about your current health and fitness level before engaging in the strength training exercises listed in this book.

## Basic Exercise Physiology

Have you ever wondered why muscles grow or how strength gains happen? It's not magic; it's science. As you lift, push, and pull, your muscles respond, adapt, and become the horsepower that propels you forward. But here's the important thing–not all muscles are the same. They come in different shapes and sizes, each with a unique role. You've got the powerhouses like your quadriceps and hamstrings in your legs, the sculptors like your biceps and triceps in your arms, and the stabilizers that keep you balanced and upright.

Adding resistance to a workout, whether lifting weights, pulling cables or using your body weight, creates tiny tears in muscle fibers–don't worry, it's a good thing. As your body repairs these tears, *your muscles grow back stronger and more resilient.*

But muscles need energy to perform and to repair. We will talk about nutrition in future chapters. But for now, know that the primary fuel that keeps the muscles going all day long is called adenosine triphosphate (ATP). When you start moving, your body breaks down ATP, releasing the energy needed for muscle contractions. Three different systems in the body work to create fuel for muscles:

- Phosphagen system – energy-storing compounds in muscle cells that can quickly release ATP as needed.
- Glycolysis (lactic acid system) – a large store of complex carbohydrates (glycogen) in muscles from the food you eat that is used to make ATP and produces lactic acid as a byproduct.
- Aerobic respiration is the body supplying glycogen to muscles through the bloodstream. Requires a constant supply of oxygen to create ATP for extended physical activity.

When muscle cells need energy, they break down phosphates to create adenosine diphosphate (ADP). When cells have excess energy, they form ATP from ADP for future use. It's a constant cycle – push/pull, break down ATP, recharge, and repeat.

*Strength Training Myths*

Let's talk about some of the myths surrounding strength training:

**Myth: Strength Training Stunts Growth in Teens**
Reality: Properly supervised and executed strength training helps growth in teenagers. In fact, it can promote healthy bone development and enhance overall physical well-being.

**Myth: Strength Training is Unsafe for Teens**
Reality: Strength training can help teenagers improve sports performance, prevent injuries, and foster a foundation for lifelong fitness.

**Myth: Teens Should Avoid Weightlifting Until They're Fully Grown**
Reality: Considering individual maturity and fitness levels, teens can engage in weightlifting. Resistance training can be adapted to accommodate different age groups and skill levels.

**Myth: Teens Should Only Focus on Cardio for Fitness**
Reality: While cardiovascular exercise is essential, incorporating strength training into a teen's routine offers a range of benefits, including improved muscular strength, endurance, and overall physical fitness.

### Myth: Strength Training Will Make You Bulky

Reality: Similar to adults, achieving significant muscle mass requires specific conditions, including hormonal factors. Teens engaging in strength training are more likely to experience improved muscle tone and strength rather than becoming overly bulky.

### Myth: Teens Should Lift as Heavy as Possible

Reality: Teens should follow age-appropriate strength training guidelines, emphasizing proper form and technique over lifting heavy weights. Gradual progression with lighter loads is often more suitable for their developing bodies.

### Myth: Strength Training is Only for Athletes

Reality: While beneficial for teen athletes, strength training is not exclusive to them. All teenagers can reap the rewards of improved fitness, enhanced bone health, and injury prevention through a well-designed strength training program.

### Myth: Teens Shouldn't Do Strength Training Before Puberty

Reality: Strength training can be introduced before puberty, focusing on bodyweight exercises and proper form. Starting early helps teens develop fundamental movement patterns and sets the stage for more advanced training as they mature.

### Myth: Teens Will Develop Poor Posture from Lifting Weights

Reality: When executed with proper form, strength training can improve your posture by strengthening the muscles that support the spine.

**Myth: Teens Can Skip Warm-Ups and Cool Downs**

Reality: Warming up before strength training and incorporating a cool-down afterward are crucial for injury prevention. Teens should prioritize dynamic stretches and light cardiovascular activity before and static stretches after their strength workouts.

Parents, coaches, and teenagers themselves need to be informed about the realities of strength training during adolescence. Strength training can be a safe and valuable addition to a teenager's overall fitness routine with proper guidance, supervision, and age-appropriate programming.

Now that that's out of the way let's get technical and talk about the three phases of muscle contractions:

*Types of Muscle Contractions: Eccentric, Concentric, and Isometric*

1. **Eccentric Contractions:** When the muscle lengthens under tension. Think of this as the lowering phase of a bicep curl or the descent during a squat. Don't be fooled – this phase is just as crucial as the others.
2. **Concentric Contractions:** The muscle shortens, generating force to move a weight or your body. Think of this as the lifting phase of a bicep curl or the ascent during a squat.
3. **Isometric Contractions:** Have you ever held a plank or paused at the bottom of a squat? That's isometric. The muscle stays the same length, working to maintain position.

## Difference Between Strength Training and Isometric Exercises

This is a tale of two techniques, each with its unique impact on your muscles and connective tissue. Strength training involves dynamic movement, the ebb and flow of muscle lengthening and contracting, while isometric exercises focus on static positions, engaging muscles without significant joint movement.

If you incorporate isometric exercises into your strength training routine, you will progress to heavier weights and greater overall strength faster than if you performed strength training alone. Neglecting isometrics can potentially lead to more injuries as you force your bones and muscles to lift heavier and heavier weights without strengthening the tendons and ligaments that hold those together and provide the utmost flexibility to your connective tissues. Here are the key differences between strength training and isometric exercises:

| | Strength Training | Isometric Exercises |
|---|---|---|
| **Muscle Contraction** | Muscles contract and lengthen through a range of motion. This can include exercises like weightlifting, where the muscles work against an external force, causing them to contract and relax. | These involve static muscle contractions without significant joint movement. Muscles are engaged, but the length of the muscle doesn't change. |

| Range of Motion | It often involves a full range of motion, where muscles go through both the concentric (shortening) and eccentric (lengthening) phases during an exercise. | These exercises focus on maintaining a specific position or angle without moving the joint, so there is no range of motion. |
|---|---|---|
| Equipment and Resistance | Typically, it involves the use of external resistance, such as free weights, machines, resistance bands, or body weight. | They often require little to no equipment, as they rely on the body's resistance or static positions against an immovable object. |
| Joint Movement | It involves dynamic joint movement, and exercises can be designed to target specific muscle groups through a variety of motions. | Focus on static positioning and minimal joint movement during the exercise. |
| Time Under Tension | Involves varying time under tension, with different phases of muscle contraction and relaxation. | Typically, it involves a sustained contraction for a set period without changing muscle length. |

| Application | It is often used for overall muscle development, improving strength, and enhancing functional fitness. | It is commonly employed for rehabilitation, improving joint stability, and developing static strength in specific positions. |
| --- | --- | --- |
| **Effect on Cardiovascular System** | It can contribute to cardiovascular health indirectly through increased metabolism and calorie expenditure. | They may have less impact on the cardiovascular system as they do not involve continuous, dynamic movement. |

It's worth noting that including both strength training and isometric exercises in a well-rounded fitness routine can provide a comprehensive, targeted approach to your muscle development. Remember to always prioritize proper form and technique and listen to your body. Be prepared to adjust the resistance as needed. Consistency and good form are the keys to activating different aspects of muscle function, tendon and ligament strength, and overall fitness.

# Chapter 2: Safety, Recovery, and Avoiding Injury

Welcome to the combat training ground! Now that you're suited up, we need to get the safety brief out of the way before we run out onto the field. Here, we will cover warm-ups and cool-downs, proper form, the importance of recovery, and avoiding the pitfalls that can quickly throw you off your game.

DON'T SKIP THIS CHAPTER! Many people create the terrible habit of just blowing this stuff off as non-important. Those are the people who end up getting injured, hitting plateaus in their training, and wishing they'd paid attention in class.

### The Importance of the Warm-Up and Cool-Down

These pre- and post-exercise rituals enhance performance, prevent injuries, and promote overall well-being. Let's delve into why incorporating warm-up and cool-down routines is critical.

A proper warm-up gradually increases your heart rate and blood flow throughout the body, which prepares your cardiovascular system for upcoming physical activity. It consists of light physical activity (running in place or knee raises) and stretching. This increases flexibility, preparing your body for more strenuous movements and reducing the risk of strains and sprains. It also helps to mentally prepare you for the workout you're about to perform.

On the flip side, a good cool-down helps your body gradually decrease your heart rate, preventing dizziness or fainting that can occur when you abruptly stop intense exercises. This is simply reducing the intensity of any exercises you've been doing, such as going from a run or jog into a walk, and again, some stretching to help flush away waste byproducts such as lactic acid in the muscles. Finally, it can contribute to better joint health, reducing the risk of injuries over time.

### The Importance of Proper Form

Think of proper form as your armor – it's not just for show; it's your protection against injuries. When you lift weights or engage in isometric exercises, doing it with the correct form ensures that you're targeting the right muscles and not putting unnecessary stress on joints or ligaments. Typically this is keeping your back straight and abdominal muscles tight during the movements. Not all for exercises, but this advice works for most.

Using proper form means learning to do each exercise correctly. The better your form, the better your results. If you need to figure out if you're doing an exercise correctly, ask someone. Proper form also means not holding your breath. You should breathe out as you push a weight up and breathe in as you let it back down.

Whether you're squatting, bench pressing, or holding a plank, pay attention to your form—it's the key to exercising safely. Start each movement slowly, try to feel which muscles are working, and imagine them contracting as you lower or raise the weight. Do the same for the reverse movement. Never rush through exercises or swing your body as you are performing them.

> **PRO TIP:** If you can't lift a heavy amount of weight without swinging your body or contorting it into awkward positions... you're doing it wrong!

Selecting appropriate weight for strength training is a crucial step in ensuring a safe and effective workout. The goal is to challenge your muscles without compromising form or risking injury. It's really about self-evaluating your current fitness level and realizing that if you're starting out, you're not going to be able to lift as heavy as the person who's been doing this for a while. It's also about setting realistic goals. It takes time, dedication, and other variables to see the results you want to see.

You're going to get buff after a few months, and you're going to be able to bench 3x your weight in a few months.

*Guidelines to help you select appropriate weights:*

**Start Light:** If you're new to strength training, start with lighter weights. This allows you to focus on proper form and technique.

**Choose a Weight that Challenges You:** The right weight should feel challenging but manageable.

**Listen to Your Body:** Pay attention to how your body responds during and after each set. If the weight is too heavy, your form may suffer. If it's too light, you won't feel challenged.

**Maintain Proper Form:** Form should always take precedence over the amount of weight you're lifting. If you can't maintain good form, the weight is likely too heavy.

**Progress Gradually:** As you become stronger, gradually increase the weight to continue challenging your muscles. Consistent progress is key to seeing improvements.

**Use a Spotter if Needed:** For some exercises, such as with free weights like the bench press, having a spotter can provide safety and confidence to lift slightly heavier weights. Just make sure they're not on their phone!

Remember, the key is to find the right balance between challenging yourself and maintaining good form. It's a journey of gradual progress, so be patient and don't hesitate to make adjustments as needed. Consult with a fitness professional or trainer if you need clarification on the appropriate weights for your specific goals and fitness level.

*Why Recovery Matters*

Now, let's talk about the downtime between your workouts – recovery. Your muscles need time to heal and rebuild. It's during this recovery period that the real magic happens. Sleep becomes your sidekick, aiding in muscle repair and overall well-being. Just like recharging after a boss battle, your body also needs time to recuperate. So, embrace rest days, prioritize sleep, and let your body do its repair work behind the scenes. Your body not only repairs muscles in your sleep, but it also burns calories after a day of tearing muscle fibers.

I must emphasize the importance of getting a good night's sleep to take full advantage of your body's autophagy. What is the world is that word? It basically means your body's process of breaking down old cell parts so your body can operate more efficiently. It's like the body's natural recycling process that begins when cells are stressed, damaged, or just old and stop functioning correctly.

## *Avoiding Common Mistakes*

Like me, many people learn the hard way. And it's usually the common mistakes that keep you from reaching your goals. Let's talk about some of these.

It's tempting to go all out every day, but overtraining can lead to fatigue, decreased performance, and even injuries. Listen to your body, and give it the rest it deserves. Not all pain is gain: If you're feeling sharp or persistent pain during an exercise, it's a red flag! Stop, reassess your form, and consult with a fitness professional if needed.

You probably have yet to see an athlete prepare for a workout or sporting event by kicking back and watching everyone else stretch. That's because by the time they get where they are in their career, they know a proper warm-up prepares their muscles for the work ahead, and a cool-down helps prevent stiffness and aids in recovery.

And, of course, it goes without saying there's a higher level of maturity expected than when you're chilling with friends. Hurting yourself or someone else because you're goofing around or not paying attention is no laughing matter.

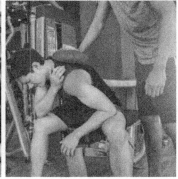

Remember, this journey is about longevity and resilience. Proper form, prioritizing recovery, and avoiding common mistakes are your allies in this adventure. So, suit up, pay attention to the details, and let's make sure your journey is one of strength, not setbacks. Onward to a safer, stronger you!

# Chapter 3: Nutrition for Strength and Growth

As mentioned before, strength training is not just about lifting weights. In this chapter, we're going to discuss how it's a holistic transformation that involves both sweat in the gym and a mindful approach to nutrition. As you sculpt your physique and build strength, the role of a proper diet becomes paramount. In this chapter, we will explore the intricate relationship between nutrition and strength training, the nutrients essential for growth, the impact of hydration on performance, and the crucial role of proteins, carbohydrates, and fats in fostering muscle, tendon, and ligament development.

One important caveat—I am not a licensed nutritionist. So, just as you would consult your primary care physician before engaging in any strenuous workout routines, such as strength training, you should also speak with them about a diet plan that works for you.

### Understanding the Synergy: Strength Training and Nutrition

Strength training is more than a series of exercises; it's a physiological combo that demands fuel and sustenance. Your body is an ever-changing machine, and the proper nutrients act as the building blocks for growth and recovery. A good diet is the bedrock upon which your strength gains are built.

Your body requires an adequate number of calories for fuel during strength training. This doesn't mean a free pass to indulge in empty calories; it means providing your body with the energy it needs to perform and recover. Timing is everything, especially in the world of strength training. Pre-workout nutrition primes your body for the upcoming session, ensuring optimal performance. Post-workout nutrition becomes the bridge between exhaustion and recovery, kickstarting the repair and growth processes.

You may be familiar with the term macronutrients. These are essential nutrients your body requires to support its various functions. Let's talk about these a little so you understand why they say a balanced diet is necessary for growth.

### Carbohydrates: Energizing the Journey

Carbohydrates are your body's primary and most efficient energy source, providing fuel for various bodily processes like physical activity and the functioning of organs. They provide the energy for intense workouts and replenish your muscles' glycogen stores post-exercise. Having sufficient glycogen stores contributes to overall endurance and allows for optimal performance during strength training, as these exercises often involve short bursts of intense effort.

Carbs also play a crucial role in the recovery process after workouts. If your carb stores are low, the body may resort to breaking down muscle tissue for energy. There are two types of carbs you'll hear about in the nutrition realm. Complex carbohydrates and simple carbohydrates.

Complex carbs include whole grains, fruits, and vegetables because they have a more intricate chemical structure and take longer for the body to digest and absorb, leading to a more gradual and sustained release of energy. Simple carbs (such as sodas, fruit juices, snacks, and sweets) are called this because they have a much simpler chemical structure and are quickly digestible, providing only quick bursts of energy. You can see why they are definitely not the best source of carbohydrates for strength training. So, it's recommended you opt for complex carbohydrates to provide sustained energy.

### *Proteins: The Architects of Muscle Growth*

Proteins are the undisputed heroes in the strength training saga. In case you didn't know, proteins are the architects responsible for repairing and building muscle tissue. When you eat protein, your body breaks it down into amino acids, which are used to repair and build new muscle tissue. Athletes engaged in strength training often require higher protein intake to support their muscle development and recovery.

If you are engaged in intense strength training but you're not consuming an adequate amount of protein in your diet, you can run the risk of muscle protein breakdown and loss of healthy muscle tissue. So it goes without saying you should ensure an adequate intake of high-quality protein sources such as lean meats, dairy, eggs, and plant-based options like beans and quinoa if you want your muscles to repair and grow.

*Fats: The Silent Strength*

Fats often play a backstage role, but their significance in strength training is profound. In fact, fats play several roles in supporting strength training and overall athletic performance. Healthy fats help hormone production, including testosterone—the key hormone for muscle protein synthesis and strength gains. Fats are also essential components of your body's cell membranes and, therefore, particularly important for muscle cells during workout recovery.

Most people don't know that fats provide more than twice the energy per gram compared to carbohydrates and proteins. So, adequate fat intake, along with carbs and protein, will help fuel prolonged workouts. We will talk about micronutrients in a quick second but know that some vitamins (such as A, D, E, and K) are called fat-soluble because they are dissolved in fat and stored in the body's fat tissues.

However, the quality of the fats consumed matters. It is recommended that you incorporate healthy fat sources like avocados, nuts, seeds, and olive oil. Saturated and trans fats, found in certain processed foods, should be limited for lifelong health.

## Micronutrients: The Unsung Heroes

While macronutrients take center stage, micronutrients play a vital supporting role. Some key roles of micronutrients include:

- B Vitamins play a huge role in the conversion of macronutrients into energy, called energy metabolism.
- Calcium, magnesium, and potassium are crucial for muscle function and repair and are also known as *electrolytes*.
- Vitamin D and K are essential for maintaining bone density and strength, which are required to withstand the pressure placed on them during strength training.
- Iron, B12, and Folate are significant players in the transport of oxygen in the blood and in the production of red blood cells.
- Vitamin C, E, Selenium, and Zinc are antioxidants that help neutralize free radicals in the body.
- Vitamin D and Zinc are also involved in hormone regulation related to muscle function and growth.

> *Free radicals are unstable molecules that seek out electrons from other molecules, causing a chain reaction known as oxidative stress.*

- Vitamins A, C, D, and Zinc are essential for immune function, helping maintain the integrity of the skin—a primary barrier against infections.
- Vitamins B1, B6, and B12 play a vital role in nervous system function, neuromuscular coordination, and overall muscle function.

So, as you can see, a balanced diet, including macronutrients as well as an ample supply of vitamins and minerals through a diverse array of fruits and vegetables, will contribute to overall health, immunity, and efficient bodily functions.

*Water: The Silent Performer*

Hydration isn't just about satisfying thirst; it's a performance enhancer. Even mild dehydration can impair strength, power, and endurance. Maintaining optimal fluid balance is crucial for sustained energy during workouts. During intense workouts, your body heats up. Adequate hydration facilitates efficient temperature regulation through sweat, preventing overheating and promoting optimal performance.

Post-exercise, rehydration is vital for recovery. It aids in nutrient transport, reduces muscle soreness, and supports the repair processes initiated by strength training.

*Beyond Muscles: Nourishing Connective Tissues*

Strength training doesn't solely target muscles; it places stress on tendons and ligaments. These connective tissues play a critical role in joint stability and overall strength. Proper nutrition is the key to ensuring their health and resilience.

While protein is celebrated for muscle growth, its importance extends to tendons and ligaments. But did you know that collagen is a protein abundant in connective tissues that requires amino acids from dietary protein sources for synthesis? Incorporating collagen-rich foods into your diet provides those necessary building blocks for the connective tissues. Foods like bone broth, fish, and collagen supplements can support tendon and ligament health.

# Chapter 4: Mental Strength and Well-Being

I n the realm of strength training, the mind is just as significant as the muscles it guides. Beyond the physical transformations, there lies a powerful synergy between strength training and mental well-being. This chapter unravels the concept of mental toughness, explores the psychological benefits embedded in the iron-clad journey, and delves into the profound impact on confidence and self-esteem. Moreover, we will navigate the delicate balance between academics, sports, and strength training, providing recommendations for a holistic approach to well-being.

*Mental Toughness and Sports Psychology*

Mental toughness is the resilient mindset that enables individuals to navigate challenges, setbacks, and adversity with composure and determination. It's not just about enduring the physical demands of strength training but about fortifying the mind to embrace the journey, both its triumphs and tribulations.

In the gym, mental toughness takes center stage. You're impressed by those who can push through fatigue, overcome self-doubt, and stay committed to the pursuit of strength. Even so, strength training becomes a training ground for the mind, sculpting resilience and cultivating mental conditioning essential for athletic success. In the realm of sports psychology, the common threads in all mental conditioning are the techniques specifically designed to enhance focus, manage stress, and foster the mental toughness required to navigate the challenges of competitive sports.

In the weight room and on the field, adversity is like a forge that shapes character. You must view setbacks as opportunities for growth. Think of setbacks as milestones on the road to greatness. You have to achieve these milestones before moving on to the next mission. Don't think of setbacks as disappointments. The sooner you learn to fail and get back up, the sooner you learn the valuable lesson each of these setbacks has to teach you and improve your game.

The path to true strength is paved with challenges. You must foster a mindset that thrives amidst adversity. Whether that is conquering a personal record in the gym or excelling in a competition, the ability to envision success is a lethal weapon in the arsenal of the mind. Each small victory contributes to an unshakeable confidence that becomes the bedrock of enduring mental toughness.

> **True strength extends beyond the physical—**
>
> **it resides in the resilience of the mind.**

## *Beyond the Physical: Nourishing the Mind*

Strength training acts as a release valve for the pressures of daily life. Lifting weights provides a meditative focus, reducing stress and fostering mental clarity. The gym becomes a sanctuary where the mind finds solace amidst the challenges of the outside world.

Engaging in strength training triggers the release of endorphins, the body's natural mood enhancers. These neurotransmitters not only alleviate stress but induce a sense of euphoria, contributing to an overall positive mental state.

Quality sleep is a cornerstone of mental well-being. Strength training promotes better sleep patterns, ensuring that the mind undergoes the necessary restoration for optimal cognitive function and resilience.

## *Empowerment from Within*

The physical gains achieved through strength training serve as tangible evidence of capability. As individuals witness their bodies becoming stronger and more resilient, a parallel transformation occurs within the realm of self-esteem and confidence.

Each successful lift, each conquered challenge in the gym, becomes a metaphor for overcoming obstacles in life. The sense of accomplishment derived from navigating the rigors of strength training instills a belief in one's ability to face challenges head-on.

Strength training encourages a shift in focus from aesthetics to functionality. Embracing the strength and capabilities of the body fosters a positive body image, contributing to heightened self-esteem and self-worth.

## *The Art of Juggling Priorities*

Balancing academics, sports, and strength training requires adept time management. Establishing a schedule that accommodates study sessions, athletic commitments, and gym sessions is essential. Prioritize tasks based on urgency and importance.

Integrating strength training into a busy schedule requires strategic planning. Opt for shorter, high-intensity workouts that maximize efficiency. Designate specific days for strength training and tailor routines to align with academic and sports commitments.

Strength training serves as more than a physical outlet; it's a mental reprieve. During breaks from academics and sports, the gym becomes a sanctuary for mental refreshment. The endorphin release and stress reduction contribute to enhanced focus and productivity.

Balancing these priorities is a formidable task, and seeking support is paramount. Communicate with coaches, teachers, and peers to create a support network that understands and respects the multifaceted nature of your commitments.

# Chapter 5: Chest Exercises and Techniques

Welcome to chest-centric strength training, where we unravel the secrets to sculpting and fortifying your pectoral muscles. In this chapter, we present a curated list of ten dynamic and ten isometric exercises tailored to amplify the strength and definition of your chest. Each exercise is accompanied by detailed instructions on proper form and techniques, ensuring a harmonious blend of safety and effectiveness in your chest training journey.

Note that the key to achieving growth and progress in your training isn't attempting to do all of these exercises at once. The idea is to choose 3 of these exercises to practice good form and create the muscle memory necessary to progress to a heavier weight in the future.

*Weight Lifting Exercises for Chest*

These exercises are going to require access to a gym, a weight bench, and/or a set of free weights. The section below on Isometric Exercises for the Chest uses your body weight and, at most, a dumbbell or two.

## 1. Barbell Bench Press

**Proper Form:**

- Lie on a flat bench, feet planted on the ground.
- Grip the barbell with hands slightly wider than shoulder-width apart.
- Lower the bar to your chest, elbows forming a 90-degree angle.
- Slowly press the bar back up to the starting position.

**Technique Tips:**

- Maintain a stable grip on the bar.
- Control the descent and ascent for maximum muscle engagement.

## 2. Dumbbell Pullover

**Proper Form:**

- Lie on a bench with only your upper back on the surface.
- Hold a dumbbell with both hands overhead.
- Lower the dumbbell behind your head, then lift it back to the starting position.

**Technique Tips:**

- Keep a slight bend in your elbows.
- Engage your chest and legs throughout the movement.

## 3. Chest Dips

**Proper Form:**
- Use parallel bars or a dip station.
- Lower your body until your upper arms are parallel to the ground.
- Push your body back up to the starting position.

**Technique Tips:**
- Lean slightly forward to target the chest more.
- Keep your elbows pointed slightly outward.

## 4. Incline Dumbbell Press

**Proper Form:**
- Set the bench to a 30-45 degree incline.
- Hold a dumbbell in each hand above your chest.
- Lower the dumbbells to chest level, then press them back up.

**Technique Tips:**
- Control the weights throughout the range of motion.
- Maintain stability by keeping your back against the bench.

## 5. Cable Crossover

**Proper Form:**
- Stand between two cable machines with cables set high.
- Grab the handles with arms extended to the sides.
- Bring your hands together in front of you, then return to the starting position.

**Technique Tips:**
- Keep a slight bend in your elbows.
- Focus on squeezing your chest at the center of the movement.

## 6. Push-Up Variations

**Proper Form:**
- Perform push-ups with different hand placements (wide, narrow, staggered).
- Maintain a straight line from head to heels.

**Technique Tips:**
- Adjust hand positions to target different parts of the chest.
- Control the descent and ascent for optimal muscle engagement.

 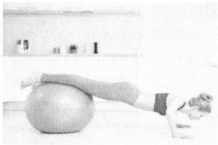

## 7. Machine Chest Press

**Proper Form:**
- Adjust the seat and handles of the chest press machine.
- Press the handles forward while seated.
- Return the handles to the starting position.

**Technique Tips:**
- Ensure a full range of motion.
- Adjust the machine to align with your chest height.

## 8. Pec Deck Machine Flyes

**Proper Form:**
- Sit on the pec deck machine with elbows bent.
- Bring the arms together in front of you.
- Return to the starting position with control.

**Technique Tips:**
- Keep a slight bend in your elbows.
- Focus on the squeeze at the center of the movement.

## 9. Medicine Ball Chest Pass

**Proper Form:**
- Stand facing a partner or wall, holding a medicine ball at chest height.

- Explosively push the ball forward, extending your arms.

**Technique Tips:**
- Choose a weight that is challenging enough to require effort but not so heavy that it compromises your form.
- Keep your movements controlled to prevent overextension or hyperextension of the arms.

10. **Decline Bench Press**

**Proper Form:**
- Set the bench to a decline angle.
- Grip the barbell with hands slightly wider than shoulder-width.
- Lower the bar to your chest and press it back up.

**Technique Tips:**
- Ensure your feet are securely positioned.
- Control the movement to avoid excessive arching.

## Isometric Exercises for Chest

These exercises are mostly bodyweight exercises, with a few that use dumbbells or even resistance bands that can be bought online in lieu of a weight bench and set of free weights. Remember, the goal of isometric exercises is the prolonged hold. Putting pressure on the muscles and holding the position strengthens your tendons and ligaments while working the muscles.

### 1. Wall Press Isometric Hold

**Proper Form:**
- Stand facing a wall with palms pressed against it.
- Apply force against the wall and hold.

**Technique Tips:**
- Maintain constant tension in the chest.
- Focus on pressing through the palms.

### 2. Push-Up Hold

**Proper Form:**
- Hold the lowest position of a push-up.
- Keep your body in a straight line.

**Technique Tips:**
- Engage your chest and core throughout.
- Breathe steadily during the hold.

## 3. Dumbbell Chest Squeeze

**Proper Form:**
- Lie on a bench with a dumbbell in each hand.
- Squeeze the dumbbells together at chest level.
- Hold the squeeze for a set duration.

**Technique Tips:**
- Maintain a steady squeeze without straining.
- Control the release of the dumbbells.

## 4. Resistance Band Chest Press Hold

**Proper Form:**
- Anchor a resistance band to a stationary object.
- Hold the ends of the band at chest height.
- Press outward against the resistance and hold.

**Technique Tips:**
- Adjust band tension for appropriate resistance.
- Focus on the chest contraction.

## 5. Chest Flye Isometric Hold

**Proper Form:**
- Lie on a bench with dumbbells in hand.
- Lower the dumbbells to chest level.
- Hold the position without touching the chest.

**Technique Tips:**
- Keep a slight bend in the elbows.
- Feel the stretch in the chest muscles.

## 6. Bodyweight Chest Squeeze

**Proper Form:**
- Stand with arms extended forward at chest height.
- Squeeze your chest muscles together.

**Technique Tips:**
- Emphasize the contraction in the chest.
- Hold the squeeze for a set duration.

## 7. Resistance Band Chest Press Hold

**Proper Form:**
- Set up the bands at chest height.
- Hold the bands, arms extended.
- Press outward against the bands and hold.

**Technique Tips:**
- Adjust body angle for varied resistance.
- Control the movement for stability.

## 8. Isometric Chest Dips

**Proper Form:**
- Perform chest dips but hold at the lowest position.
- Keep upper arms parallel to the ground.

**Technique Tips:**
- Engage chest muscles to hold the position.
- Control the descent and ascent.

## 9. Stability Ball Chest Squeeze

**Proper Form:**
- Lie on a stability ball with a dumbbell in each hand.
- Squeeze the dumbbells together above your chest.

**Technique Tips:**
- Use a stable ball for a better range of motion.
- Keep the core engaged for stability.

## 10. Plate Squeeze Isometric Hold

**Proper Form:**
- Hold a weight plate between your hands at chest level.
- Squeeze the plate with force and hold.

**Technique Tips:**
- Choose an appropriate weight for your strength.
- Focus on the chest contraction.

# Chapter 6: Arm Exercises and Techniques

In this chapter, we'll explore a list of 10 strength training exercises, accompanied by proper form and techniques, designed to enhance the strength and definition of your arms and shoulders. Additionally, we'll review ten isometric exercises, focusing on static contractions to target and fortify these muscle groups and the tendons and ligaments that support them.

*Arm and Shoulder Exercises*

**1. Bicep Curl with Barbell**

**Proper Form:**
- Stand with feet shoulder-width apart, holding a barbell with palms facing forward.
- Curl the barbell toward your shoulders, keeping elbows close

to your body.

- Lower the barbell with control.

**Technique Tips:**

- Keep your back straight and core engaged.
- Avoid using momentum; focus on controlled movements.

## 2. Tricep Dips

**Proper Form:**

- Sit on a bench and grip the edge with hands shoulder-width apart.
- Slide your hips off the bench, lowering your body.
- Press back up using your triceps.

**Technique Tips:**

- Keep your elbows close to your body.
- Lower until your elbows are at a 90-degree angle.

## 3. Hammer Curls with Dumbbells

**Proper Form:**

- Hold a dumbbell in each hand with palms facing your body.
- Curl the dumbbells toward your shoulders.
- Lower the dumbbells with control.

**Technique Tips:**

- Maintain a neutral grip throughout.
- Focus on the brachialis and brachioradialis muscles.

## 4. Shoulder Press with Barbell

**Proper Form:**
- Stand or sit with a barbell at shoulder height.
- Press the barbell overhead, fully extending your arms.
- Lower the barbell back to shoulder height.

**Technique Tips:**
- Keep your core engaged for stability.
- Avoid arching your back during the press.

## 5. Concentration Curls with Dumbbell

**Proper Form:**
- Sit on a bench, holding a dumbbell in one hand.
- Rest your elbow on the inside of your thigh.
- Curl the dumbbell toward your shoulder.

**Technique Tips:**
- Isolate the bicep by preventing body movement.
- Control the movement for maximum effectiveness.

## 6. Lateral Raises for Shoulders

**Proper Form:**
- Hold a dumbbell in each hand by your sides.
- Lift the dumbbells laterally until they reach shoulder height.
- Lower the dumbbells with control.

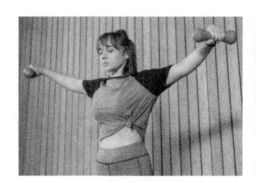

**Technique Tips:**
- Keep a slight bend in your elbows.
- Focus on engaging the lateral deltoids.


## 7. Skull Crushers for Triceps

**Proper Form:**
- Lie on a bench, holding an EZ bar or dumbbells.
- Lower the weight toward your forehead, keeping your elbows stationary.
- Extend your arms back to the starting position.

**Technique Tips:**
- Control the descent to avoid strain on the elbows.
- Use a spotter for added safety.

## 8. Front Raises for Anterior Delts

**Proper Form:**

- Hold a dumbbell in each hand with palms facing your body (alternately, you can also use a kettlebell).
- Lift the dumbbells forward until they reach shoulder height.
- Lower the dumbbells with control.

**Technique Tips:**

- Maintain a slight bend in your elbows.
- Focus on contracting the front deltoids.

## 9. Preacher Curls with EZ Bar

**Proper Form:**

- Sit at a preacher's bench, holding an EZ bar.
- Curl the bar toward your shoulders.
- Lower the bar with control.

**Technique Tips:**

- Keep your upper arms against the preacher's bench.
- Emphasize the contraction in the biceps.

## 10. Reverse Flyes for Rear Delts

**Proper Form:**

- Bend at the hips, holding a dumbbell in each hand.
- Lift the dumbbells laterally, focusing on the rear delts.
- Lower the dumbbells with control.

**Technique Tips:**

- Keep a slight bend in your elbows.
- Squeeze your shoulder blades together at the top.

## Isometric Arm and Shoulder Exercises

### 1. Wall Sit with Bicep Curl Isometric Hold

**Proper Form:**
- Perform a wall sit.
- Hold a dumbbell in each hand, performing a bicep curl.
- Hold the contraction for a set duration.

**Technique Tips:**
- Keep knees at a 90-degree angle.
- Squeeze the biceps throughout.

### 2. Plank with Tricep Squeeze

**Proper Form:**
- Assume a plank position.
- Squeeze your triceps, holding the contraction.
- Maintain a straight line from head to heels.

**Technique Tips:**
- Engage your core for stability.
- Focus on contracting the triceps.

### 3. Isometric Hold with Hammer Curl

**Proper Form:**
- Perform a static lunge.
- Hold a dumbbell in each hand, performing a hammer curl.
- Hold the contraction for a set duration.

**Technique Tips:**
- Keep a 90-degree angle in the lunge.
- Emphasize the contraction in the brachialis.

## 4. Shoulder Isometric Hold with Resistance Band

**Proper Form:**
- Anchor a resistance band at hip height.
- Hold the band with both hands, arms extended.
- Squeeze your shoulders, holding the contraction.

**Technique Tips:**
- Adjust band tension for resistance.
- Focus on the lateral deltoid contraction.

## 5. Tricep Extension Hold

**Proper Form:**
- Assume a chair pose position.
- Hold a dumbbell with both hands overhead.
- Lower the dumbbell behind your head and hold.

**Technique Tips:**
- Keep your back straight during the pose.
- Engage the triceps throughout.

## 6. Isometric Concentration Curl

**Proper Form:**
- Sit on a bench, holding a dumbbell in one hand.
- Perform a concentration curl and hold.
- Emphasize the bicep contraction.

**Technique Tips:**
- Prevent body movement for isolation.
- Hold the contraction at the top of the curl.

## 7. Plank with Lateral Raise Hold

**Proper Form:**
- Assume a plank position.
- Hold a dumbbell in each hand, lifting laterally.
- Hold the lateral raise at shoulder height.

**Technique Tips:**
- Engage your core for stability.
- Focus on the lateral deltoid contraction.

## 8. Isometric Tricep Dips

**Proper Form:**
- Perform tricep dips.
- Hold the lowest position.
- Keep your elbows close to your body.

**Technique Tips:**
- Engage your triceps for the hold.
- Control the upward and downward motion.

## 9. Isometric Front Raise with Resistance Band

**Proper Form:**
- Stand on a resistance band.
- Hold the band with both hands, arms extended.
- Lift the band forward, holding the contraction.

**Technique Tips:**
- Adjust band tension for resistance.
- Focus on contracting the anterior deltoid.

## 10. Isometric Overhead Press with Dumbbells

**Proper Form:**
- Sit or stand, holding a dumbbell in each hand.
- Press the dumbbells overhead and hold.
- Maintain a straight line from wrists to elbows.

**Technique Tips:**
- Engage your shoulders and triceps.
- Control the descent of the dumbbells.

# Chapter 7: Leg Exercises and Techniques

Prepare to strengthen and sculpt the foundation of your physique with a carefully curated selection of dynamic strength training exercises for the lower body. In this chapter, we'll explore ten powerhouse exercises designed to target your legs and enhance overall lower body strength. Additionally, we'll delve into ten isometric exercises, focusing on static contractions to fortify and tone those essential muscle groups.

*Lower Body Strength Exercises*

**1. Barbell Back Squat**

**Proper Form:**
- Position a barbell across your upper back.
- Stand with feet shoulder-width apart.
- Lower your body by bending at the hips and knees.
- Press back up to the starting position.

**Technique Tips:**
- Keep your back straight and chest up.
- Ensure your knees track over your toes.

## 2. Deadlifts

**Proper Form:**
- Stand with feet hip-width apart, holding a barbell in front.
- Hinge at your hips, lowering the barbell toward the ground.
- Engage your glutes and hamstrings to return to a standing position.

**Technique Tips:**
- Maintain a neutral spine throughout.
- Keep the barbell close to your body.

## 3. Lunges with Dumbbells

**Proper Form:**
- Hold a dumbbell in each hand at your sides.
- Take a step forward, lowering your back knee toward the ground.
- Push off your front foot to return to the starting position.

**Technique Tips:**

- Ensure your front knee stays above your ankle.
- Keep your torso upright during the lunge.

## 4. Leg Press Machine

**Proper Form:**

- Sit on a leg press machine with feet on the platform.
- Push the platform away, extending your legs.
- Bend your knees to lower the platform back down.

**Technique Tips:**

- Adjust the machine for proper leg extension.
- Keep your back against the seat.

## 5. Bulgarian Split Squats

**Proper Form:**

- Stand a few feet from a bench or elevated surface.
- Place one foot behind you on the bench.
- Lower your body into a lunge position.

**Technique Tips:**

- Lower your back knee toward the ground.
- Maintain balance throughout the movement.

## 6. Calf Raises

**Proper Form:**
- Stand with feet hip-width apart.
- Lift your heels off the ground by pushing through the balls of your feet.
- Lower your heels back down.

**Technique Tips:**
- Squeeze your calf muscles at the top.
- Perform the exercise on a flat surface.

## 7. Box Jumps

**Proper Form:**
- Stand in front of a sturdy box or platform.
- Jump onto the box, landing softly.
- Step back down and repeat.

**Technique Tips:**
- Land with knees slightly bent.
- Use your arms for momentum.

## 8. Romanian Deadlifts

**Proper Form:**
- Hold a barbell in front of your thighs.
- Hinge at your hips, lowering the barbell toward the ground.
- Engage your hamstrings and glutes to return to a standing position.

**Technique Tips:**
- Keep a slight bend in your knees.
- Maintain a straight line from head to hips.

## 9. Step-Ups with Dumbbells

**Proper Form:**
- Hold a dumbbell in each hand at your sides.
- Step onto a bench or elevated surface.
- Push through your top foot to stand upright.

**Technique Tips:**
- Ensure your entire foot is on the bench.
- Control the movement throughout.

## 10. Seated Leg Curl Machine

**Proper Form:**
- Sit on a leg curl machine with the pad against your lower legs.
- Curl the pad toward your glutes by flexing your knees.
- Extend your legs back to the starting position.

**Technique Tips:**
- Adjust the machine for proper range of motion.
- Keep your back against the seat.

## *Isometric Lower Body Exercises*

### 1. Wall Sit with Leg Extension Hold

**Proper Form:**
- Perform a wall sit.
- Extend one leg forward and hold the position.
- Alternate legs for a set duration.

**Technique Tips:**
- Keep your back against the wall.
- Engage your quadriceps during the extension.

### 2. Isometric Lunge Hold

**Proper Form:**
- Step forward into a lunge position.
- Hold the lunge at the lowest point.
- Maintain balance and stability.

**Technique Tips:**
- Ensure your front knee is above your ankle.
- Engage your glutes for added stability.

### 3. Isometric Sumo Squat Hold

**Proper Form:**
- Perform a sumo squat by standing with feet wide apart.
- Lower your body into a squat position.
- Hold the squat at the lowest point.

## STRENGTH TRAINING FOR TEENS

**Technique Tips:**
- Keep your knees tracking over your toes.
- Engage your inner thighs during the hold.

## 4. Single-leg isometric Deadlift

**Proper Form:**
- Stand on one leg, hinging at your hips.
- Lower your upper body toward the ground.
- Hold the position with a straight back.

**Technique Tips:**
- Keep your non-standing leg extended behind.
- Focus on balance and hamstring engagement.

## 5. Isometric Calf Raise Hold

**Proper Form:**
- Perform a calf raise.
- Hold the raised position at the top.
- Squeeze your calf muscles during the hold.

**Technique Tips:**
- Lift your heels as high as possible.
- Maintain stability during the hold.

## 6. Seated Isometric Leg Press Hold

**Proper Form:**
- Sit on a leg press machine.
- Set the weight to a challenging level.
- Press the platform and hold the position.

**Technique Tips:**
- Keep your back against the seat.
- Focus on contracting your quadriceps.

## 7. Isometric Lateral Leg Raise Hold

**Proper Form:**
- Lie on your side, supporting your upper body with your elbow.
- Lift your top leg laterally and hold.

**Technique Tips:**
- Keep your hips stacked for stability.
- Engage your outer thigh during the hold.

## 8. Isometric Step-Up Hold

**Proper Form:**
- Step onto a bench or elevated surface.
- Hold the top position of the step-up.

**Technique Tips:**
- Ensure your entire foot is on the surface.
- Engage your glutes during the hold.

## 9. Isometric Bulgarian Split Squat Hold

**Proper Form:**
- Perform a Bulgarian split squat.
- Hold the lunge at the lowest point.

**Technique Tips:**
- Lower your back knee toward the ground.
- Engage your quadriceps and glutes.

## 10. Isometric Leg Extension Hold

**Proper Form:**
- Sit on a leg extension machine.
- Extend your legs and hold the position.

**Technique Tips:**
- Adjust the machine for proper alignment.
- Control the movement during the hold.

# Chapter 8: Back and Abdominal Exercises and Techniques

O k, it's time to learn how to fortify your core and sculpt a resilient back. In this chapter, we'll explore ten exercises targeting your back and abdominal muscles. Additionally, we'll discuss ten isometric exercises to build endurance and definition in these crucial muscle groups.

*Dynamic Back and Abdominal Exercises*

**1. Deadlifts**

**Proper Form:**

- Stand with feet hip-width apart, holding a barbell in front.
- Hinge at your hips, lowering the barbell toward the ground.
- Engage your back muscles to return to a standing position.

**Technique Tips:**
- Maintain a neutral spine throughout.
- Keep the barbell close to your body.

## 2. Lat Pulldowns

**Proper Form:**
- Sit at a lat pulldown machine, gripping the bar with wide hands.
- Pull the bar down to your chest, engaging your lat muscles.
- Release the bar back up with control.

**Technique Tips:**
- Keep your chest up and shoulders down.
- Control the movement throughout.

## 3. Renegade Rows

**Proper Form:**
- Begin in a plank position with a dumbbell in each hand.
- Row one dumbbell to your hip while balancing on the other.
- Alternate sides for each repetition.

**Technique Tips:**
- Keep your body in a straight line.
- Engage your core for stability.

## 4. Hyperextensions (Back Extensions)

**Proper Form:**
- Lie face down on a hyperextension bench.
- Lift your upper body and legs off the ground.
- Lower back down with control.

**Technique Tips:**
- Squeeze your lower back muscles at the top.
- Maintain a straight line from head to heels.

## 5. Seated Cable Rows

**Proper Form:**
- Sit at a cable row machine, holding the handles with an overhand grip.
- Pull the handles toward your torso, squeezing your shoulder blades.
- Extend your arms back to the starting position.

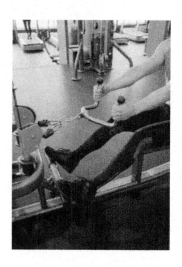

**Technique Tips:**
- Keep your back straight and chest up.
- Focus on the contraction in your mid-back.

## 6. Russian Twists

**Proper Form:**

- Sit on the ground, leaning back at a 45-degree angle.
- Hold a weight or medicine ball with both hands.
- Rotate your torso, bringing the weight to each side.

**Technique Tips:**

- Engage your core throughout the rotation.
- Keep your feet off the ground for an added challenge.

## 7. Face Pulls with Resistance Band

**Proper Form:**

- Anchor a resistance band at face height.
- Grab the band with both hands and pull toward your face.
- Control the release back to the starting position.

**Technique Tips:**

- Keep your elbows high during the pull.
- Focus on contracting your upper back muscles.

## 8. Plank

**Proper Form:**

- Start in a plank position on your forearms.
- Maintain a straight line from head to heels.
- Hold the plank for a set duration.

**Technique Tips:**
- Engage your core and glutes.
- Avoid sagging or lifting your hips.

## 9. Bent Over Rows with Dumbbells

**Proper Form:**
- Hinge at your hips, holding a dumbbell in each hand.
- Row the dumbbells toward your hips, squeezing your back.
- Lower the dumbbells with control.

**Technique Tips:**
- Keep your back flat and chest up.
- Focus on the contraction in your lats.

## 10. Hanging Leg Raises

**Proper Form:**
- Hang from a pull-up bar with an overhand grip.
- Lift your legs toward the ceiling, engaging your lower abs.
- Lower your legs back down with control.

**Technique Tips:**
- Avoid swinging; use controlled movements.
- Squeeze your abs at the top of the lift.

## Isometric Back and Abdominal Exercises

### 1. Isometric Plank Row

**Proper Form:**
- Start in a plank position with a dumbbell in each hand.
- Row one dumbbell to your hip, keeping your body still.
- Hold the rowed position for a set duration.

**Technique Tips:**
- Engage your core for stability.
- Keep your hips parallel to the ground.

### 2. Isometric Superman Hold

**Proper Form:**
- Lie face down on the ground.
- Lift your arms, chest, and legs off the ground.
- Hold the Superman position for a set duration.

**Technique Tips:**
- Squeeze your lower back and glutes.
- Keep your head in a neutral position.

## 3. Isometric Reverse Plank

**Proper Form:**
- Sit on the ground with hands behind you, fingers pointing toward your feet.
- Lift your hips toward the ceiling, creating a straight line.
- Hold the reverse plank for a set duration.

**Technique Tips:**
- Engage your core and glutes.
- Keep your shoulders down and chest lifted.

## 4. Isometric L-Sit Hold

**Proper Form:**
- Sit on the ground with your legs extended.
- Lift your legs off the ground, forming an "L" shape.
- Hold the L-sit for a set duration.

**Technique Tips:**
- Keep your back straight and chest lifted.
- Engage your core throughout.

## 5. Isometric Woodchopper Hold

**Proper Form:**
- Hold a weight or medicine ball with both hands.
- Rotate your torso and lift the weight to one side.
- Hold the woodchopper position for a set duration.

**Technique Tips:**
- Engage your obliques during the hold.
- Maintain a controlled rotation.

## 6. Isometric Leg Scissors

**Proper Form:**
- Lie on your back with your legs extended.
- Lift one leg toward the ceiling while lowering the other.
- Hold the leg scissors for a set duration.

**Technique Tips:**
- Keep your lower back pressed into the ground.
- Engage your lower abs throughout.

### 7. Isometric Single-Arm Plank

**Proper Form:**

- Start in a plank position on one forearm.
- Lift your opposite arm toward the ceiling.
- Hold the single-arm plank for a set duration.

**Technique Tips:**

- Engage your core and glutes.
- Keep your body in a straight line.

### 8. Isometric Bicycle Crunch Hold

**Proper Form:**

- Lie on your back with hands behind your head.
- Lift one leg while bringing the opposite elbow toward it.
- Hold the bicycle crunch position for a set duration.

**Technique Tips:**

- Engage your core and twist from your torso.
- Keep your lower back on the ground.

### 9. Isometric Bridge Hold

**Proper Form:**

- Lie on your back with your knees bent and feet flat.
- Lift your hips toward the ceiling.
- Hold the bridge position for a set duration.

**Technique Tips:**

- Squeeze your glutes at the top.
- Keep your back straight during the hold.

## 10. Isometric Side Plank with Rotation

**Proper Form:**
- Start in a side plank position on your forearm.
- Rotate your torso, bringing your top arm under your body.
- Hold the rotated side plank for a set duration.

**Technique Tips:**
- Engage your obliques during the rotation.
- Keep your hips lifted and body aligned.

# Chapter 9: Integrating Strength Training into Sports

In this chapter, we explore the impact that a well-structured strength training program can have on enhancing sports performance. From the underlying principles that fuel athletic success to sport-specific exercises and drills, this chapter serves as your guide to unleashing the power of strength in the realm of sports.

*The Foundation: Understanding Strength Training for Sports*

Integrating strength training into sports necessitates a solid understanding of its fundamental principles. Strength training is not simply about lifting weights; it is a strategic and purposeful approach to developing the physical attributes crucial for athletic success.

### The Power of Functional Strength

Central to any successful strength training program for sports is the cultivation of functional strength. Unlike isolated strength, functional strength is dynamic and transferable to the specific movements and demands of your sport. Functional strength is truly the framework upon which physical competence stands. It includes flexibility, mobility, and a mind-body connection to synchronize mental focus with physical actions.

At the heart of functional strength lies a resilient core—an area often associated solely with abdominal muscles. In reality, the core includes the entire trunk of the human body and the full torso, including the back and hips. Strengthening this central powerhouse not only fortifies posture but acts as a stabilizing force, fostering balance and preventing injury.

### Building Explosive Power

Explosive power is the secret weapon of many elite athletes. This training typically includes drills tailored to ignite your fast-twitch muscle fibers. By harnessing explosive power, you'll amplify your ability to sprint, jump, change direction, and execute quick, decisive movements crucial in various sports scenarios.

Think of the speed and agility a wide receiver needs as he dodges back and forth, running, leaping, and spinning across the field to avoid the defensive linebackers who are charging at him full speed with one intent—to knock him to the ground. It's all about the coordination of split-second decisions, quick directional changes, and dynamic movements that breed unparalleled athleticism.

This is where the fast-twitch muscle fibers come into play. They are designed for rapid contractions and bursts of force. Plyometrics training can be the key to unlocking this explosive potential. Plyometrics includes exercises such as box jumps, depth jumps and medicine ball throws to generate maximal force in minimal time.

*Examples of Sport-Specific Exercises and Drills*

Understanding that each sport demands unique skill sets, let's talk about some sport-specific exercises and drills designed to elevate your performance in specific athletic domains.

**Soccer: Agility, Endurance, and Striking Power**

Soccer demands a unique blend of speed, agility, and endurance. Cone drills, shuttle runs, and ladder drills become indispensable tools for soccer enthusiasts, fostering rapid footwork and the ability to navigate the pitch with agility and precision.

**Basketball: Vertical Jump, Speed, and Defensive Agility**

For aspiring basketball players, explosive vertical jumps and lightning-quick lateral movements are non-negotiable. Plyometric drills like box jumps and agility ladder exercises take center stage, enhancing not only leaping ability but also the agility crucial for swift changes in direction during a game.

## Track and Field: Sprinting, Jumping, and Throwing

Track and field athletes navigate the relentless pursuit of speed and explosive power. Sprint jumps and hurdle drills become cornerstones of their training regimen. The track becomes a canvas where each explosive step and powerful leap is a testament to the precision of sport-specific training.

## Baseball/Softball: Rotational Power, Arm Strength, and Speed

In the realm of bat and ball sports, explosive rotational power is the name of the game. Medicine ball twists, rotational lunges, and cable woodchoppers amplify the strength of the core and lower body, providing the foundation for powerful swings and throws.

## Gymnastics: Strength in Flexibility

For gymnasts, strength is inseparable from flexibility and precision. Targeted exercises such as bodyweight movements, flexibility drills, and apparatus-specific strength training refine their ability to execute gravity-defying routines with grace and strength.

## Strength Training with Sport-Specific Development

This section bridges the gap between strength training and the intricacies of your chosen sport. We'll explore strategies for integrating strength workouts seamlessly into your existing training schedule, ensuring a synergistic relationship between your strength gains and sport-specific skills.

### Periodization for Peak Performance

Periodization is a strategic approach to training that optimizes your physical capabilities at critical points in your sports season. Whether you're gearing up for competition or entering an off-season phase, learning how to tailor your strength training program for peak performance is essential to athletic success. Focusing your strength training on distinct aspects of strength, power, and skill development will allow you to excel in many areas simultaneously.

### Injury Prevention and Rehabilitation

Strength training isn't just about performance enhancement; it's a potent tool for injury prevention and rehabilitation. You have to be used to listening to your body and pushing only when your body says push and pulling back when it tells you to. Take your time, take things slow, and learn how to hear your body tell you when an activity is too much for it to handle. Only then can you reduce the risk of injuries and expedite the recovery process, keeping you in the game for the long haul.

# Chapter 10: Beyond High School—Lifelong Fitness

**W**elcome to the final chapter of this book. Here, I help you bridge the transition from adolescent strength training to embracing lifelong fitness. As you step into adulthood, the principles you've cultivated in your formative years will serve as the cornerstone for sustained health and vitality. In this chapter, we'll explore the seamless integration of strength training into your adult life, highlighting the profound connection between strength, longevity, and overall well-being. Let's learn how to foster a sustainable fitness routine that propels you toward a vibrant and active future.

## Transitioning from Teen to Adult Strength Training

The first step in the transition is acknowledging the natural changes your body undergoes as you move into adulthood. You'll experience changes in areas such as metabolism, muscle development, hormonal shifts, and recovery dynamics. This understanding lays the foundation for tailoring your strength training approach to align with your evolving needs.

The transition to adult strength training is a marathon, and as any athlete, body-builder, or decathlon winner can attest—strength is a journey, not a destination. You must also refine your training to align with holistic well-being. We've focused a lot in this book on proper form and isometric exercises for a reason—preserving joint health becomes much more critical as you age.

Adults face unique challenges in maintaining bone density and joint health. Lifelong strength training becomes a potent ally in warding off conditions like osteoporosis and arthritis. It's more important to perform exercises specifically tailored to fortify your skeletal structure and promote joint longevity.

## Setting Realistic Goals for Adulthood

As an adult, your fitness goals will undoubtedly shift from those of your teenage years. Setting realistic expectations is the foundation for a sustainable and fulfilling strength journey. Whether your focus is on maintaining muscle mass, improving cardiovascular health, or simply staying active, you will soon learn that strength training isn't just about building muscles; it's a holistic approach that benefits your cardiovascular system.

There is a symbiotic relationship between strength training and heart health. You'll seek new routines that enhance circulation, regulate blood pressure, and contribute to overall cardiovascular well-being. As metabolism naturally undergoes changes with age, maintaining a healthy weight becomes a priority. You'll also need to explore strength training's role in managing weight, boosting metabolism, and navigating the intricacies of adult nutrition.

*Developing a Sustainable Fitness Routine: The Art of Balance*

Adulting comes with its own set of responsibilities and time constraints. Whether you're juggling work, family, or other commitments, you'll soon learn the beauty of efficiency in your workouts and how consistency trumps intensity in the long run. Many adults experiment to develop a strategic selection of exercises that deliver maximum impact in minimal time. High-intensity interval training (HIIT), compound movements, and functional exercises become stalwarts, ensuring that each workout is a potent investment in health without sacrificing time.

Although it may sound boring now, as an adult, you may explore mindful recovery practices—maybe through yoga, meditation, or rejuvenating activities. Understanding how to fuel your body for sustained energy, optimal performance, and overall well-being will become crucial.

Learn to prioritize fitness as a non-negotiable aspect of self-care. It will be a mental exercise to overcome the illusion of time scarcity and cultivate a discipline to prioritize health amidst the myriad demands of adulthood. But as you build a network of encouragement through workout buddies or virtual accountability partners, the collective strength becomes a source of motivation, ensuring that the journey is not walked alone.

Sustainability in fitness is not just about the destination but the journey itself. You must learn the art of reflection, celebrating the progress made, and embracing the continual evolution of your fitness routine.

# Thank you!

I hope you enjoyed reading this book. I hope that it has helped you learn in your journey to a stronger you! If it has helped at all, I'd appreciate an honest review on Amazon so others know how much you liked it. Thank you, so much, and good luck, with your strength training journey!

https://mybook.to/Strength

— Thomas Allen

# References

*10 effective isometric workouts to boost muscle building.* (2018, April 7). Indian Workouts - Home GYM, Martial Arts and Exercises. https://www.indianworkouts.com/isometric-workouts/

Allison, L. (2022, November 14). *What happens to your muscles during exercise and recovery?* Longevity.Technology Lifestyle | Health, Fitness & Technology. https://longevity.technology/lifestyle/what-happens-to-your-muscles-during-exercise-and-recovery

Fetters, K. A. (2023, March 22). *Post-Workout Muscle Recovery: How to let your muscles heal and Why.* EverydayHealth.com. https://www.everydayhealth.com/fitness/post-workout-muscle-recovery-how-why-let-your-muscles-heal/

Hargreaves, M., & Spriet, L. L. (2020). Skeletal muscle energy metabolism during exercise. *Nature Metabolism,* 2(9), 817–828. https://doi.org/10.1038/s42255-020-0251-4

Hörst, E. (2023, December 7). *Training with Long-Duration Isometric Exercises.* Training for Climbing - by Eric Hörst.

https://trainingforclimbing.com/training-with-long-duration-isometric-exercises/

*Isometric training for youth athletes - Sportsmith.* (2022, December 6). Sportsmith. https://www.sportsmith.co/articles/isometric-training-for-youth-athletes

Jackson, D. (2017, April 3). *Types of muscle contraction - HSC PDHPE.* HSC PDHPE. https://pdhpe.net/the-body-in-motion/how-do-the-musculoskeletal-and-cardiorespiratory-systems-of-the-body-influence-and-respond-to-movement/muscular-system/types-of-muscle-contraction/

Lanese, N. (2021, October 16). Stunning images show how muscles heal themselves after a workout. *livescience.com.* https://www.livescience.com/muscle-repair-by-roaming-nuclei

McCoy, J., & CPT, C. S. (2023, August 4). 12 plyometric exercises to build explosive strength and crank up your workout's intensity. *SELF.* https://www.self.com/story/a-10-minute-fat-burning-plyometric-workout-you-can-do-at-home

Newton, P. (2020, July 23). *6 exercises for improving your mental toughness.* Strategic Athlete. https://strategicathlete.com/6-exercises-improving-mental-toughness/

*Nutrition rules that will fuel your workout.* (2021, February 23). Mayo Clinic. https://www.mayoclinic.org/healthy-lifestyle/nutrition-and-healthy-eating/in-depth/nutrition-rules-that-will-fuel-your-workout/art-20390073

OlympiaFitness. (2022, May 6). *Isometric exercises to improve athletic performance | Olympia Fitness + Performance.* Olympia Fitness + Performance. https://olympiafitnessri.com/isometric-exercises-to-improve-athletic-performance

*OpenAI.* (n.d.). https://www.openai.com/

Professional, C. C. M. (n.d.-a). *Autophagy.* Cleveland Clinic. https://my.clevelandclinic.org/health/articles/24058-autophagy

Professional, C. C. M. (n.d.-b). *Lactic acid.* Cleveland Clinic. https://my.clevelandclinic.org/health/body/24521-lactic-acid

*Weight training: Do's and don'ts of proper technique.* (2022, November 29). Mayo Clinic. https://www.mayoclinic.org/healthy-lifestyle/fitness/in-depth/weight-training/art-20045842

*Why isometric exercises belong in your workout routine - Dr. Axe.* (2023, November 25). Dr. Axe. https://draxe.com/fitness/isometric-exercises

Printed in Great Britain
by Amazon